TO PAT & MAYMAY —
HOPE YOU ENJOY THE BOOK ...
& DIG THOSE ABC'S!
LOVE,
Neil

D0947502

"GET inside the MUSIC & Listen."
Thelonius Monk

THE JAZZ ALPHABET

A PERSONAL LOOK at 26 JAZZ GREATS from A to Z

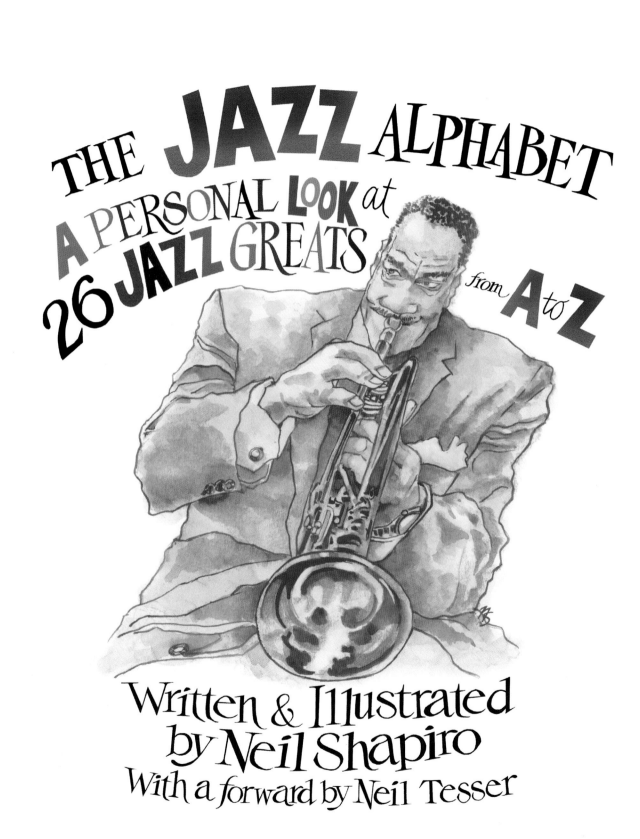

Written & Illustrated by Neil Shapiro
With a forward by Neil Tesser

Pictured on title page: Buck Clayton.

To my brother Gerry and my wife Maureen. Gerry encouraged
me to love writing, and Mo encouraged me to love jazz.

Forward

In December 2016, Neil Shapiro approached me at a holiday party with a question: Did I know of any jazz musicians whose surnames began with "X?"

After determining that Neil spelled his own first name correctly, I happily shared the name that immediately came to mind—Ed Xiques. Obviously. Xiques is a journeyman saxophonist who graced the sensational Thad Jones/Mel Lewis Orchestra in the 1970s, and who has gone on to related careers as a composer and educator. (And the answer really was more obvious than you might think, since Xiques is the only musician that any jazz aficcionado can identify who would fit Neil's qualification.)

But now, I needed to find out: *Why such an odd question in the first place?*

Neil explained to me his plans for the book in your hand—a "Jazz Alphabet" populated by his portraits and brief personalized descriptions of the musicians pictured. I liked the idea quite a bit, and was happy to have provided one small if somewhat valuable piece of information.

I'm even happier now that the book has arrived.

Like jazz itself, Neil's work takes liberties in the service of greater expressivity. These are not "perfect" likenesses, tracing the exact line of Miles Davis's furrowed brow, or Red Norvo's trim goatee, or Charlie Parker's plump fingers; we have photography for that. These are something better. They fall between portraiture and caricature, occupying a middle ground that allows Neil to capture essences—the creativity, personality, and even the soul of his subjects. In illustrating the uniquness of his subjects, they exhibit his own individuality in equal measure.

Look closely enough and you can hear the music.

       —*NEIL TESSER, Grammy-winning author, critic, and broadcaster*

I can't think of jazz without thinking of Louis Armstrong. With his galvanizing technique and his "direct emotional intensity" (as William Gottlieb put it in *The Golden Age of Jazz*), Armstrong stamped jazz with his personality from the moment he stepped on the stage. As famous as he got (and Satchmo got really famous), by all accounts he remained an easily approached, open and earthy man. "Jazz is played from the heart," he said. "You can even live by it. Always love it."

A is for Louis Armstrong

"HOT can be COOL, & COOL can be HOT, & EACH can be BOTH. BUT HOT or COOL, MAN, JAZZ is JAZZ."

When jazz pianist William James Basie found himself stuck in Kansas City in the mid '20s (the traveling vaudeville show he was playing with abruptly disbanded) he discovered the sound and the genre that would define his career: Big Band music. A radio DJ later nicknamed him "Count", and the Count Basie orchestra ultimately defined Big Band music at its best.

On *A Love Supreme,* John Coltrane does these wild improvisations on a basic melody that, to me, sound like he's trying out ideas. It's the sound of a musician thinking — raw and fascinating.

C is for John Coltrane

"My music is the Spiritual EXPRESSION of WHAT I AM: my FAITH, my Knowledge, MY BEING."

I first heard *Kind of Blue* more than 40 years ago on a rainy Sunday afternoon in Chicago. I put down the book I was reading and the music seeped into me. I didn't find out until later that it was one of the best selling jazz albums of all time. All I knew then was, Miles Davis defined cool. He still does.

D is for Miles Davis

"Sometimes you HAVE to PLAY a long time to be able to PLAY like YOURSELF."

Duke Ellington turned down an art scholarship to Pratt Institute. And he dropped out of Armstrong Manual Training School, where he was studying commercial art. Why? Because he loved music more. After more than 1,000 compositions over 50 years—the largest recorded personal jazz legacy—it seems he made the right choice.

E is for Duke Ellington

"By & Large, JAZZ HAS ALWAYS BEEN like the KIND of MAN You wouldn't want your DAUGHTER to ASSOCIATE WITH."

Listening to Ella Fitzgerald, I always feel her own pleasure in her voice. Whether scatting or singing Cole Porter, she's having a great time, and we're invited to the party. I accept her invitation.

F is for Ella Fitzgerald

"The ONLY thing Better than SINGING is MORE SINGING."

B eyond giving what is the best portrayal of a jazz musician I've ever seen—Dexter Gordon, basically playing himself in Bertrand Tavernier's film *Round Midnight*—it's such a pleasure listening to Gordon slide in and around a melody. He does it with smooth control.

G is for Dexter Gordon

"Jazz to ME is LIVING MUSIC. It's a music that since its BEGINNING (has) EXPRESSED the feelings, the DREAMS, HOPES of the People."

The tremulous vulnerability in Billie Holiday's voice is unique. Even while she balances on the edge of seeming despair, there's a sly promise of pleasure in there. How does she do that?

Whether Chuck Israels is playing with Bill Evans or, later, with his own orchestra, I'm struck by the suppleness (the only word I can think of) in both his playing and his arranging. A British jazz commentator once said of Israels that he was "a superb technician who handles the double bass as easily as if it were a guitar... Chuck Israels is one of the reasons why musicians have come reeling away from performances by the Bill Evans Trio in a mood poised between elation and utter despair."

My first reaction to hearing Illinois Jacquet was, "Man, that is one honking saxophone." From his extraordinary, influential solo on the Lionel Hampton orchestra's recording of *Flying Home,* through his associations with a succession of stellar jazz artists—among them Cab Calloway, Charles Mingus, and Count Basie—to his own Illinois Jacquet Big Band, which he led from 1981 until his death in 2004, he maintained a fierce, raw quality to his playing that was (to me, anyway) unique. Interesting fact: Jacquet played *C-Jam Blues* with President Bill Clinton on the White House lawn during Clinton's inaugural ball in 1993.

J is for ILLINOIS JACQUET

"The PATTERNS of BIG BAND MUSIC ARE smooth & CLASSICAL. IT'S GOT TO BE FRESH. The BRASS SECTION should CRACKLE, like the sound of EGGS BEING DIPPED INTO HOT GREASE."

W atching Gene Krupa play the drums is pure joy. He throws himself, his whole body, into the exercise. He attacks the drums, he caresses the drums, he celebrates the drums. And in the process, he seems to lose himself to the drums.

K is for Gene Krupa

"I think at one time, every DRUMMER wanted to Play Like KRUPA ..."
—BUDDY RICH

Yusef Lateef can be mellow when he plays the tenor sax, or sinuous when he plays the oboe or the flute or the bassoon. But he didn't stop with those; his embrace of non-Western instruments like the bamboo flute, shanai, even the shofar, led his obituary in *The New York Times* to state that Lateef "played world music before world music had a name."

L is for Yusef Lateef

"EXTERNAL INSTRUMENTS are only EXTENSIONS of the BIOLOGICAL INSTRUMENT."

Listening to Thelonius Monk is not always easy. His improvisational approach to the piano was the result of countless hours of musical exploration; he was often revisiting groupings of notes he'd already ordered.

"When you understand the inside, the outside will be just fine," he'd say. "Get inside the music and listen."

M is for
Thelonious
Monk

"JAZZ is
FREEDOM.
YOU *think*
about
THAT."

In later life, Red Norvo was a model citizen, but earlier in his career that wasn't always true. On one occasion, when his employer was showing a top executive around the NBC studios in Chicago where Norvo worked, they found him sleeping under a piano. When his boss shook him, Norvo mumbled, "Not now, honey. Got to get to rehearsal in the morning." By the late '50s he had given up drinking and smoking. Red Norvo went on to absorb and play the modern jazz of the '50s and '60s with the same ease and imagination that had already given him his moniker: Mr. Swing.

When she sings *Tea For Two,* Anita O'Day's voice skips across the musical accompaniment like a stone skipping across a lake. Her elastic, improvisational vocalizing shattered the traditional image of "the girl singer;" she was a hip jazz musician, as hip as anyone in any of the groups with whom she performed. And perform she did, well into her '80s.

When I listen to Charlie Parker, his joyfully brilliant improvisation makes his alto sax seem like it's talking to me. If I just listen hard enough, it will all become clear. It never does become clear, just more enjoyable the longer I listen.

Parker had a lot of personal demons weighing him down, but when he played he was lighter than air.

P
is for Charlie
Parker

"IF you don't LIVE IT, it won't come OUT of your HORN. They teach you there's A BOUNDARY LINE to MUSIC. But MAN, there's NO BOUNDARY LINE to ART."

After hearing Ike Quebec on *Blue & Sentimental,* a listener said, "Oh man, this tone is beautiful. I can imagine sitting on a park bench in New Orleans at night in the rain and watching a woman I love kissing another man on the street corner."

Now that is some evocative music.

Q is for Ike Quebec

"...QUEBEC had a BIG BREATHY sound that was DISTINCTIVE & EASILY RECOGNIZABLE..."
MUSIC CRITIC ALEX HENDERSON

I don't think you can talk about Django Reinhardt without talking about the raging fire that burned his left hand; burned it so badly that he had to learn a whole new fingering system built around the two fingers on the hand that had full mobility. But when I listen to Reinhardt, I'm not thinking about that. I'm in a small French cafe, sipping wine. His one-of-a-kind improvisational guitar playing transports me to a time and place as much as any music I've ever heard.

R is for Django Reinhardt

"JAZZ ATTRACTED ME BECAUSE IN IT I found A FORMAL PERFECTION & instrumental PRECISION THAT I ADMIRE in CLASSICAL MUSIC, BUT WHICH POPULAR MUSIC doesn't HAVE."

I've listened to a lot of performers sing *Lush Life,* Billy Strayhorn's masterpiece. From Ella Fitzgerald to Frank Sinatra to Johnny Hartman to Billy Eckstine, they're all wonderful. But for some reason it's Strayhorn's own version that stays with me. His voice is thin and unremarkable, but it's that raw, unvarnished quality that haunts me:

> *"...Romance is mush / Stifling those who strive /*
> *I'll live a lush life / In some small dive / And there I'll be /*
> *While I rot with the rest / Of those whose lives are lonely, too"*

Billy Strayhorn was a teenager when he wrote it.

S is for Billy Strayhorn

"Billy Strayhorn was MY RIGHT ARM, my LEFT ARM, all the EYES in the BACK of my HEAD, My BRAINWAVES in HIS HEAD, & HIS in MINE."
DUKE ELLINGTON

When Jack Teagarden sings, he's got a lazy, lived-in sound that seems to flow out of him naturally (when he sings with Louis Armstrong on *Old Rockin' Chair,* their voices blend like scotch and soda). And when he puts the trombone to his lips, that relaxed quality continues to flow. It's anything but lazy, however.

T is for Jack Teagarden

"ALL THAT I'VE PLAYED, All THAT I'VE SUNG, I couldn't HAVE DONE any other WAY."

I am used to hearing violin in the context of a classical orchestra. When Michal Urbaniak plays, the sound is not pretty. It's raw, vital, and alive with feeling.

I listen to him with new ears.

U is for Michal URBANIAK

ABANDONED the VIOLIN for the SAXOPHONE, but RETURNED to it when HE RETURNED to POLAND. HAS played with CHICK COREA, QUINCY JONES, & WEATHER REPORT.

On a live recording of *Willow Weep For Me*, Sarah Vaughan blends what sounds like a microphone drop or a stumble into her performance with an intimate ease that pulls the audience in. She ends by singing that she "really fouled up this song real well" and the audience eats it up.

Why shouldn't they? Every note is gorgeous!

V is for Sarah Vaughan

"There are NOTES BETWEEN NOTES, You Know."

Listening to Mary Lou Williams, whether early in her career (she began in 1922, at the age of 12) or later, her confidence comes through loud and clear. On *Free Spirits,* from 1975, her playing takes your breath away.

W is for Mary Lou Williams

"ANYTHING you ARE SHOWS UP in your MUSIC — JAZZ is WHATEVER you ARE, PLAYING yourself, BEING yourself, LETTING your THOUGHTS COME THROUGH."

My career in advertising afforded me the chance to observe countless session musicians at work. Not well known to the general public, they turned in flawless performances and earned the admiration of their colleagues, with whom they shared an easy camaraderie. Saxophonist/composer Ed Xiques fits that description. Best known for his time with the Thad Jones/Mel Lewis Orchestra, he's worked with artists across the musical spectrum, from Frank Sinatra to The Jackson Five. For the last couple of decades he's been the resident composer with Diane Moser's Composer's Big Band, which recently held a tribute concert in his honor. As Ms Moser put it, "We love his stories and his wonderful spirit."

X is for Ed XiqueS

"I started LISTENING to JAZZ on the RADIO in the 1950s... the FIRST RECORDING I purchased was DUKE ELLINGTON ("ELLINGTON UPTOWN")... a very SPECIAL RECORDING."

A music critic once called Lester Young "the original hipster," and it's hard to argue with that. No one talked like Prez did, no one dressed like he did, and his light, feathery tenor sax playing was unique. When he begins playing *Mean to Me* on Art Ford's All-Star Jazz Party in 1958, he appears frail.

But his final notes? A swinging triumph.

Y is for Lester Young

"We were ALL influenced by Lester... NOBODY'S got what he's GOT. HE'S STILL the DADDY."

—ZOOT SIMS

On Miles Davis's *In a Silent Way,* Joe Zawinul composed the title cut. His ethereal keyboard playing is utterly haunting. I later learned that he was picked to participate the night before the recording session, and was asked to "bring music."

He brought it, all right.

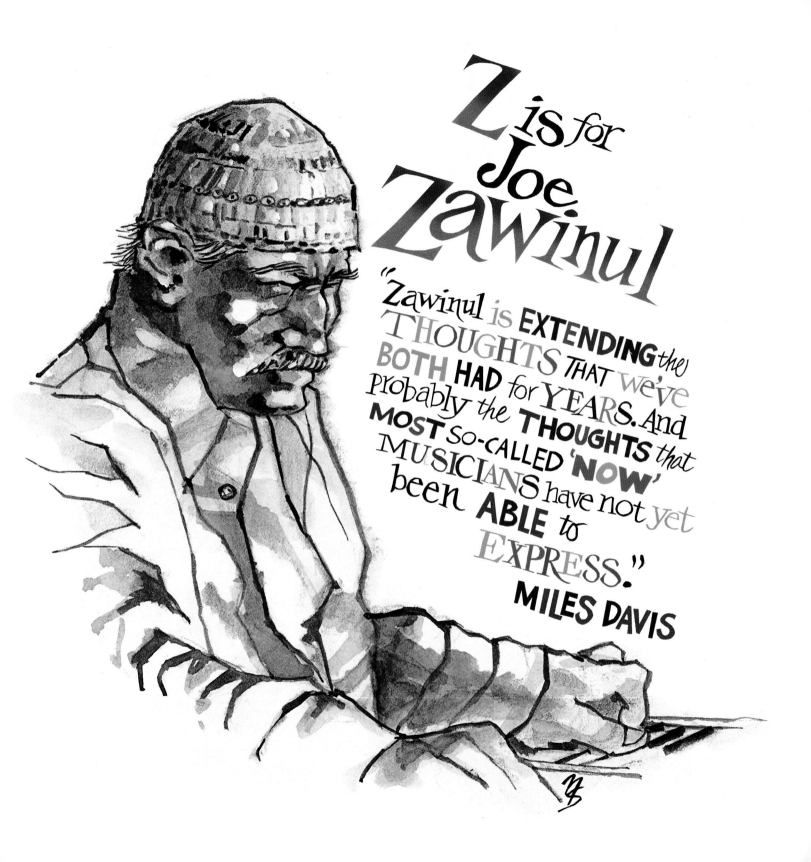

Z is for Joe Zawinul

"Zawinul is EXTENDING the THOUGHTS THAT we've BOTH HAD for YEARS. And probably the THOUGHTS that MOST so-called 'NOW' MUSICIANS have not yet been ABLE to EXPRESS."

MILES DAVIS

A Final Thought

From Gene Ammons to Denny Zeitlin, there are numerous other choices for a Jazz Alphabet. Not just who to choose, but why? What instruments? How many vocalists? What genre? What era? After all, jazz covers a lot of territory. That could be seen as a problem.

I see it as an opportunity. When I create more Jazz Alphabet portraits, I listen to more jazz. And as Art Blakey said, "Jazz washes away the dust of everyday life."

Acknowledgments

oward the end of my career in advertising, I went back to school, and got a master's degree in illustration from Syracuse University. The Independent Studies Program there was run by Murray Tinkelman, who encouraged us to follow our passion when searching for subject matter to illustrate. I did just that when I completed a class assignment by creating a portrait of John Coltrane. That's where the idea for the Jazz Alphabet was born. Murray died in 2016, but he left an indelible mark on me. I can't thank him enough.

As my initial sense of what the Alphabet should be went through several early iterations, my good friend Ted Naron helped me enormously. His graceful writing informed my own approach, and his musical knowledge was invaluable.

I could not have completed this book without the collaboration of graphic designer Cliff Questel. His adeptness at all things digital guided me through myriad production issues, and he brought a precise eye to the organization of the layout.

So many of my friends and family, both in the flesh and online, have given me encouragement and advice in the creation of this book. In particular, I want to thank (in no special order): Steve Woodall, Tony Gleeson, Pat Byrnes, Tom and Gary Gianni, Leif Peng, Jon Rocket, Gordon Walek, Ruth Magalian, Michael Bartlett, Larry Garrett, Patty and Scott Gustafson, Matt Ferguson, and Elaine Soloway. They all provided a helping hand (and more) when I most needed it. And to all the people I'm forgetting, my humble apologies and gratitude.

Every one of the jazz musicians depicted in this book has been an inspiration in one way or another. They all took different journeys: Some battled personal demons and others endured arbitrary societal boundaries. Some achieved success early and held onto it throughout their careers. Whatever their stories, it's their music that endures. I salute them all, from A to Z.

Throughout the exhilarating, often challenging process of creating the contents of this book, I adopted the mindset of my wife, Maureen Gorman: *Do The Work.* It sounds simple, but those three words became a life raft for me. Thank you, Mo.

Neil Shapiro loves jazz. And since he can't play or sing a note to save his life, depicting jazz artists is the best way he knows to honor the music he loves and the musicians who make it.

In a previous life Neil was an advertising art director, creating award winning campaigns for national clients such as Gatorade, McDonald's, and Cap'n Crunch.

Since then, he has created scores of editorial and advertising illustrations, and illustrated numerous children's books. Neil has taught, lectured, and written extensively on illustration and advertising design. His artwork has been exhibited in solo and group shows in Chicago and New York galleries, and he has led the design and creation of a public work of art.

Neil lives in Chicago with his wife, Maureen Gorman, and his dog, Ruka.